BREAKING THE CODE

Becoming a Music Marketing Sniper

TABLE OF CONTENTS

INTRODUCTION

The universe of music began as an outlet for unadulterated ability. In the days of yore, individuals would sing and make music for their love. Individuals shaped gatherings, referred to today as groups or ensembles, to give other individuals incredible and legit music. As times passed by, artists were mentioned by Kings and Queens, giving a specific incentive to music and artists. This like this led artists to begin requesting an expense or for some offerings while they performed. The scene today appears universes from the music business before. Today we realize that there are considerably more undertakings, employment, and individuals, in the middle of the craftsman and the audience. Nowadays, the extent of the craftsman is more prominent, his big-name sparkles more splendid. This is the reason there is a lot of other individuals associated with the creation of music and the bundling of a craftsman. Nowadays, music has been separated into an item, and it is undoubtedly transforming into beautiful art that needs to sell, and a craftsman that can keep up his or her melodic personality while as yet having the option to sell is the thing that makes a star.

The uplifting news is, When you need to work in the music business today, there are significantly more openings for work sitting tight for you, and it is merely an issue of picking the one that is directly for your arrangement of abilities and gifts. A portion of the occupations that appear to be at the highest point of numerous individuals' rundowns is identified with music business programs. It may not look at it. However, it takes a ton of showcasing to bring a relative obscure into super fame.

Promoting assignments in the music business incorporate getting the beat of people in general. This implies, you may direct studies to find what audience members need to hear, what they make of a specific craftsman or sound, what kind of sounds are they willing to investigate, what level of the tuning in and purchasing open would bolster a particular melodic sort, and possibly how much will they pay for a tune or record. These are altogether enveloped in one territory of promoting and are incorporated into most music business programs.

Individuals in the music showcasing office additionally deal with the aggressive investigation. That is, they think about how they reasonable against their rivals, what they could improve, and what their competitors are showing improvement over them.

So how might you get in these positions? You should get into music business programs for assistance. Entry level position will find you an occupation, and interning for a particular division of any organization would serve you superior to being a general understudy. That is if you have worked under the showcasing office as an assistant, then it would be simpler for you to get contracted for a promoting position as opposed to an individual who did his entry-level posts as in a non-advertising area, or over somebody who has not had any temporary job or real involvement. Begin searching for organizations that enable you to understudy for them now. The internet is one spot you could begin, or you could visit any music-related business in your town or city. Keep in mind; however, the more engaged and concentrated your temporary job is, the more probable you will find a new line of work you need.

CHAPTER ONE

Utilizing Social Networking for Online Music Marketing

Free online music advertising procedures and information can enable people to figure out how to be perceived. If you are trying to achieve the impossible and attempting to end up acclaimed, the internet offers you an excess of instruments and techniques that you can use to advance your music.

A standout amongst the best techniques for online music promoting is video advertising. Recordings sell quick online. At YouTube and different regions online, a vast number of guests, including makers and different performers visit the website to watch recordings. By adding disks to social network locales, you can expand your opportunity of being taken note.

Software to make recordings is accessible on the Web. You can download software projects and begin building your music recordings in less time by utilizing thorough apparatuses. Other information online offers you music advertising tips, plans, methodologies, and limited time strategies that different performers used to advance their music.

You can figure out how popular and social network advertising functions. Social networks give you demonstrated approaches to communicate your music online to a massive number of users. At one time, social media was a pattern, yet today the social networks have turned out to be one of the main techniques for promoting organizations, music, or administrations.

Advertisers post information about how successful social networking is on the internet. As indicated by factual reports, around 64% of the United States internet users collaborate with client produced content. Approximately twenty-six million of the United States guests utilized Twitter. More than 220 million users from around the globe used portable social networks.

Reliable research information is accessible online. Utilizing social media to advertise your music is thriving when you use listening abilities, set up the trust, include worth, and undertaking legitimacy. Significance is set on techniques and real apparatuses you use to advance your music. The best procedures are found in social media networks.

Pepsi, as of late begun promoting in social media in the wake of finding that the social networks offered the organization a more extensive range of internet showcasing arrangements. The organization contributed millions. Pepsi hopes to increase the income of consumptions in less time significantly. Pepsi will show up in advertisements during the Super Bowl.

If you are beginning, you can't stand to burn through millions in media advertisements. Set aside cash by adding your recordings to YouTube and the social networks. Guarantee that you list your information and records in the correct classifications. If you put your music in the wrong class, the odds of getting an introduction is decreased by around 90 percent.

Studies demonstrate that individuals who include their email address and contact information in recordings increment their possibility of structure email battle records consequently if you utilize social networks for online music advertising, including your email and other contact information so makers can contact you.

Music Marketing and Promotion - What's the Difference?

What is the difference between music marketing and music advancement?

Marketing and advancement are regularly confounded among outside the box performers. There is a difference between music marketing and music advancement. Allows first to take a gander at marketing.

Marketing

Marketing is tied in with getting your objective market to know your identity, what you bring to the table, why you are putting forth it, and why what you are putting forth is something they need. Marketing is tied in with getting your objective market to know, as, and trust you.

Does your intended interest group know you? To get your objective market to identify you, they need to realize that you exist. Your accurate market needs to think about you and your music. How would you do that? You show up where they are. You should know where they hang out, what they read, where they shop, and what occasions they visit. You or your road group need a nearness before them. You can do this by performing where your objective market hangs out, posting flyers where they are at, or by having online proximity through your site and internet-based life destinations. Fundamentally, discover where your objective market hangs out and appear there!

Does your intended interest group like you? When you are before your objective market, presently you need to associate with them! Draw in with them! Care about them! Have a message and a reason that impacts them. Am I not catching that's meaning? On a personal dimension, explain to your market why you make music. What moves your music? What's the mission behind your music? On a masterful aspect, make music that they will like. Marketing is tied in withdrawing in and associating.

Does your intended interest group trust you? In some cases, you will find that once your objective market knows you and preferences you, they will presumably confide in you, yet that isn't generally the situation. During this period of marketing, your objective market is thinking: "Alright, I know your identity, and I like you, and I like your music, however, would I be able to believe that your collection or your live show will be on a par with you state it is?" Marketing is tied in with structure trust.

Music Promotion: Getting them to act.

Advancement is about conduct change. It's tied in with impacting and inducing others to act. If you have completed a fruitful occupation in your marketing, your market will say: "I know who performer X is, I like his/her music, I figure the collection will be hot." But advancement is tied in with getting them to make the following stride, understanding your market to state, "I am going to purchase the collection now." If you are marketing a live show, you need them to say, "I need to purchase tickets now." How would you get your objective market to report this? Make compelling offers! Offer limited time just limits/individual costs, special constrained release collections, music bundles, and packages.

Instructions to Market Music: An Effective No-Fail 3 Step Music Marketing Formula That Works

Step by step instructions to Market Your Music More Effectively

Realizing how to market your music is beyond question THE most significant thing you can accomplish for your music business and your music vocation in general. You know it's something that must be taken care of, and in case you're not trying endeavors to figure out how to market your music all the more adequately then you should realize that, at any rate, nothing genuine will ever occur in your music business professionals.

The principal thing to ask yourself is whether you're presently dealing with the essential components of a viable music marketing effort.

I don't get my meaning by this?

To start, it's imperative to evaluate where you're at the present moment and decide if you know and see precisely what the fundamental parts of a successful music marketing efforts are? When you plan on becoming famous in the music business; it's critical to acknowledge you'll be contributing a great deal of your time and cash into your music vocation. In case you're sure your total objective is to shape your music abilities into genuine "music business," and you have no questions about the professional way you've picked... at that point, you'll need to be as productive and gainful as you can be.

Most non-mainstream groups and performers whether from the Rock, Hip Hop, Folk or any class so far as that is concerned, will in general work on just a couple of the three necessities of successful music marketing. For example, most performers are incredible at interfacing with crowds. What with Facebook, Instagram, Twitter, and YouTube in the blend, interchanges have turned out to be stupid essential for the present artist.

Then again, requesting the deal is once in a while taken care of viable yet will, in general, be approached haphazardly and without an equation or the vital going with mindfulness battles. This need brilliance approach will result in the general hose the endeavors of even the most diligent groups and performers in the business. Lamentably, applying just one or even two of these critical segments without the third essential component in a music marketing effort won't get most extreme returns for the time contributed. This isn't the way to market music viable.

Try not to misunderstand me, getting your name out there and sharing in discussions with fans can be cold, even self-satisfying and it's unquestionably superior to not doing anything by any stretch of the imagination, yet envision the amount progressively compelling you'd be if you got down to business on these fundamental marketing parts of your music business outfitted with a recipe and a sticking point centered reason.

The Solution To Ineffective Music Marketing

When you separate the intricate details on the most proficient method to market your music adequately, it ends up evident that as an artist, it's critical to teach yourself to concentrate on the components that are most profitable for your music business development. Separated in a simple to pursue process these components of music marketing and music advancement comprise of a 3 stage equation:

Step #1 - Create Awareness: Find a crowd of people who values your music style, your sound, and your character. Make the strides essential to impart your melodic message to them. All that you do ought to make mindfulness for you and your music consistently. Approach this with exactness and a firm heading and your music business establishment will be set for quite a long time to come.

Step #2 - Connect with Your Audience: I referenced how stupid basic it is to interface with fans today. Instagram, Facebook, Twitter, YouTube, and the numerous other online "home bases" make this procedure a breeze. When you've laid the underlying foundation, and you've made your group of spectators mindful of precisely what you bring to the table, chip away at keeping up those significant on-going associations with your fans, the media and the hugely substantial music business reaches you gather en route. Your fans and contacts need to realize that you're without a doubt. That you care about them. That you're here for the whole deal, making associations with them and keeping them engaged with your development procedure will guarantee this occurs for you.

Step #3 - Sell Your Stuff (Ask for the deal): This one is fundamental. If you don't have items to sell... you DON'T have a music business. Working to make a stable, consistent cash stream for your music business is fundamental to your long haul achievement. Lure fans to spend their cash and purchase your stuff and the remainder of your music marketing procedures will stream and thrive so a lot simpler.

Truly! It's Easier Said Than Done

I perceive that it's simpler to discuss these things than it is to get them going in your vocation yet this is the thing that the music business is about so fusing these procedures into your music business crusade is an unquestionable requirement, or you basically won't keep going long enough to make scratch in the music world.

What's more, that is not what we need for your music profession.

Once more, it may appear to be simple enough to outline things out on paper, yet in all actuality, most groups and artists will locate a hundred and one different ways to mess this up.

You'll either invest a lot of energy in making mindfulness and interfacing with your group of spectators yet then neglect to request the deal. Or on the other hand, you'll require the deal approach to regularly and disregard interfacing with your kin. I referenced before that it's cool to get all gung-ho, get occupied, and head on out there and complete a lot of music marketing, however in case you're not contacting each of the three components of this procedure on the best way to market music, at that point you're feeling the loss of the vessel and all the more significantly... you're fans won't be "feeling" your vibe. They won't associate with you on a more profound dimension. Without association, there are no deals, and without sales, you don't have a music business.

Try not to Fall Into the Marketing Music Business Trap.

You've seen them. They're everywhere. They are faltering press discharges that performers love to convey these days. These press discharges are presented and carried on my inbox once a day with features like. Proceed... let it be known. You've presumably conveyed something like this yourself at some time.

Fans and media see directly through this. All the band needs are cash. For some obscure reason, the band is anticipating that us should head on over to the connection incorporated into their press discharge and snap on the purchase catch. Where's the association? Shouldn't something be said about the mindfulness we need BEFORE they request the deal?

Consider it. Have you at any point purchased a collection, or anything besides, without some passionate association? Odds are you haven't. When you think you have... reconsider it. I'm sure you'll reflect and understand that an association or some likeness thereof was unquestionably engaged with your buy. Artists who commit this indefensible marketing error ought to be embarrassed about themselves. If this is the leading way, you're advancing and marketing your music, take an hour or so to follow your outcomes.

I'm willing to wager what you find isn't empowering.

If you are Leaving Money On The Table?

Presently how about we take a gander at the other side. Shouldn't something is said about performers who associate with us magnificently however never request the deal? You've encountered it, and honestly, you likely adore them. You burrow their music, love their stage nearness, and you want to get notification from them. When you need to help them and show your affection... you don't have a clue where to go. They never reveal to you where you can purchase their stuff.

Not an incredible equation for progress, right?

If you're not requesting the deal, at that point, you're bombing your fans. Fans who love groups love to purchase "stuff" from groups. You can't fail on this. Without creating a cash stream, you basically won't prevail in the music business. It's too costly to even consider working a music business without cash stream. The fun evaporates genuine speedy when the cash continues spilling out, however never streams back in. Try not to be that band, don't be that performer.

The most effective method to Make The 3 Step Music Marketing Formula Work For You

I understand that you might not have a great deal of time in your life. You may work a 9-5 now or possibly your visiting timetable is crazy. Despite your present circumstances, it's critical to take a break to actualize these three exercises into your music business advancements. Begin by curtailing an hour of TV consistently and put that energy into making familiarity with your music.

Discover where your fans joint and get dynamic with them. Tell them what you're doing. Make some off-camera recordings on your studio recording sessions and your visiting trips in the van while in transit to your next gig. Give fans a chance to become more acquainted with your identity. Give them a chance to see you, all things considered, circumstances. This makes compatibility and association all while you construct mindfulness... one-two punch.

What do you do when you hit the washroom? Personal inquiry I know, however, stays with me for a bit. Why not take your advanced cell in with you next time and as opposed to perusing the most recent reports on Facebook, post something important on your fan page. Answer a couple of your fan inquiries on your course of events or tweet them out for anyone passing by to view. Why not share or retweet a fan post? As it were, interface with your crowd ordinarily for at any rate 15-20 minutes. Discover the time somehow.

We would all be able to discover 20 minutes in a multi-day if we need to.

Without Products You Don't Have a Music Business.

At last, requesting the deal occurs because of having items to market. Try not to have any questions yet? What are you sitting tight for? Record your live exhibitions, hit the studio, make a DVD narrative. Keep in mind if you don't have any items, and you don't have a music business. Get occupied.

When you've dealt with the mindfulness and association part of the 3 stage music marketing equation, requesting the deal is a breeze. Genuine fans genuinely DO need to purchase your stuff. When you ask without seeming pushy or greedy, they WILL buy. It's imperative to offer more mindfulness content and to interface with fans more than you request the deal, however for love... Remember to inquire.

Working these three how to market your music components viably in your profession won't just develop your music business, yet will get you headed on the correct way to making a long haul, enduring music vocation. Getting the word out (Create Awareness), assembling a fan base (Connect with Your Audience) and profiting (Ask for the Sale) will at last spot you making a course for music industry achievement.

Online Music Marketing Strategies: How Helping Others Can Help You

Online is a Very Important Tool When It Comes to Marketing

Before the web, you would need to cold pitch places out of the telephone directory and hit the asphalt in whatever climate to increase new prospects. Or on the other hand, even mail out mass amounts of postcards to get your image before the majority.

Since we can achieve on the web, one flyer posted on a web-based social networking site like Facebook or Instagram can achieve a town of individuals. This makes organizing a ton more straightforward than it used to be.

Why?

Indeed, you have the chance to find out about associations that you might not have ever found out about. There are such a significant number of clubs and gatherings that, for instance, a little Tennessee bowling group, could be found and reached.

The motivation behind why I stress this reality is because I see opportunity where others don't. Much the same as numerous independent craftsmen and groups, there isn't a boundless cash stream we can spend on anything. We set aside cash by making our very own studios, yet that $1,000 mic is, however, a far separation away, so we settle for an increasingly moderate receiver.

My point is, everybody is attempting to set aside cash, including with regard to their associations.

Imagination and Brainstorming Are the Keys to Success

Do you think a young lady scout camp hoping to do business can bear to contract Maroon 5 to compose a custom tune? Shouldn't something be said about to permit the melody? The odds are that the answer is no!!

They need to work with whatever spending they have and burning through the majority of it on music merely is not getting down to business. This applies to nearby organizations too.

The thing about everything is that with regards to publicizing, I locate that most places don't realize how to go about getting music, whether it be for foundation or a signature tune.

You need to learn how to make music as well as how to take that music and produce a salary from your music. For this situation, you realize who to target and how to ensure you both are content with the result.

How might this benefit You? Great Question...

Presently for a case of this in real life. We'll state that there is a school around the local area and they have some prevalent societies. You locate this out from digital flyers being set all over Facebook and Instagram. They are continually accomplishing something for the network, and this enables the school to increase capital.

You locate this out by visiting their site. The more individuals they have, the better it is for the crews. A thought strikes you, and you choose to make a tune about these gatherings to help spread the news about them. You incorporate essential data about every crew, in the wake of investigating, and you make it as snappy as would be prudent.

When you get the tune as extraordinary as you would you be able to converse with the music executive to make sheet music so the band can play the melody. It turns into the free tune for the crews at the school!! They choose to make a video to get the message out about how extraordinary their school organizations are.

The majority of this equitable from you finding an association and finding your way in. The best part about everything is that each school gets spending plans for specific things and music is one of them. This implies you ought to appreciate a decent check for your endeavors and backend eminences if they choose to air the video on systems. The blessing will continue giving.

No need in spending large measures of cash on a promoting organization when you could turn into your own. The significant thing for us independent specialists is to think outside the box.

With promotions everywhere tempting you to spend increasingly more, we at times overlook how amazing on the web music showcasing methodologies can be. Continuously recall that each dollar begins with an idea.

Building up Your Music Marketing Plan

As we as a whole know, a melodic profession is never beyond any doubt. This is the reason, regardless of how well we play the guitar, drums, piano, or sing; we were never urged to take on music full time. Our folks are well on the way to try and demoralize us from this way and propel us to take the more "typical" way like getting professional education and land a great job or begin a business.

Notwithstanding, music, for specific individuals, isn't only an enthusiasm; however, a calling. You can, at present, do low music maintenance. However, a few people genuinely go for handling it full time and taking on the performer's life. Perhaps it's the hero bling that is pulling them further. Maybe the pay a few stars make. Or on the other hand maybe, quite possibly, they genuinely treat music as their life.

So if you need to take on the full-time performer's way, the ideal path for you to experience it while keeping your accounts stable is to build up incredible music promoting the plan. Music showcasing is troublesome; you may need to bring about a lot of costs/ventures toward the start yet, in the long run, you will procure excellent outcomes if you go the correct way.

Besides that, music advertising likewise is tedious. You have to keep your image over individuals' heads at the specialty that you have a place with so you keep on being in the standard. You need to stay aware of the most recent patterns in promoting and clash against the top performers who have expertly made an imprint in the music business, and the individuals who genuinely have sufficient paid ability administrators to work with.

Presently, for you to not lose yourself at the intricate trap of music promoting, here are a couple of tips to have your objectives sorted out for your music showcasing plan:

In the first place, you need to begin with the general population you trust and the frameworks which worked for them. You can depend on their dedication to you to enable you to build up an extraordinary promoting procedure. When they begin discussing you and your music, individuals will, in the end, start to see it, and they will get inquisitive. From that point onward, you can likewise get them to help with the advancements. Increase their reliability. In the long run, you can extend your broadness and who knows, you may open your one of a kind fan base.

Next, when you discover the general population 's identity willing to work for the improvement of your music and your music showcasing plan, you do your exploration. The web is a comprehensive center point of data; you can do as such much while plunking down. Be available to changes and ensure that you're pushing ahead.

In conclusion, make sure to build up a framework that you find most useful and don't quit persisting. Be sorted out. Have a calendar and keep it. Track your advancement well. Numbers don't lie.

Those are the vital pieces of building up your music showcasing plan. By the day's end, set aside some effort to assess your endeavors and have a clear perspective on where you're going. Try not to dither to drop something if it doesn't work for you any longer; patterns will continue evolving. Furthermore, remember to build up your masterfulness as it is your ticket to having a fruitful performer's life.

Band Promotion - Free Music Marketing

Regardless of whether you're right now resting on your mate's love seat, you CAN advance your band with practically no cash. (You will require a PC, and we get to)

Free music advertising (as the name proposes) doesn't cost cash, yet it will take some time, imaginative and assurance. Are you game?

#1. Get an Email Account. Free email records are accessible from Gmail, Hotmail, or a great deal of other online email organizations. Just go to their landing page and sign up for a career, and you'll be up and going in minutes.

#2. Get a Soundcloud Page. You can get the band a Soundcloud page for nothing. There you can likewise load up a portion of your tunes, photographs, and so on when you have your website up email every one of your companions and fans to look at it and add them to your companion list. You would then be able to get in touch with them at the same time to report future gigs, melody discharges, and so on.

#3. Get Something to Sell. You can't profit if you don't have anything to sell. When you're playing gigs, even free ones can make you cash by offering stuff to the group of spectators. Ensure you have duplicates of your music on CD or a glimmer drive to sell. You can likewise sell the stock with your band's name and logo on it. You can do this online for nothing by setting up a virtual storefront at **CaféPress.com.** They'll give you a little storefront site and show how your logo looks on various things you select. When somebody purchases the stuff, they handle all the charging and delivering and send you a check.

#4. Get a Sponsor. Actually no, not AA support! I mean corporate help who will give your band cash to advance their organization. Begin off by searching for "Holy messenger" supports. These could be guardians, grandparents, or companions of the family who have some additional cash to put resources into your profession. At that point, hope to organizations who might profit by publicizing to the group of spectators you will play. Car sellers, garments stores, soda pop or lager wholesalers, are additionally decent prospects. Demonstrate to them that their cash will go straightforwardly into the making of the showcasing materials, and not the band brew finance! For instance, you put their logo with yours on T-shirts, flyers, blurbs, flags, and so forth., in return for them paying for the expense of making those pieces.

#5. Alert The Media. Contact local radio and TV station and offer to play any on or off-air occasions or gatherings they are having. You could get paid this time, however having your name on the brains and lips of the local movers and shakers can just assistance your vocation. With a little work, you can advertise your music for nothing and keep every one of the prizes yourself. Individuals are doing this at present, thus can you? You need to get a couple of advertising tips, traps, and systems like the master's use.

CHAPTER TWO

Sovereignty Free Music - Tips To Improve Your Marketing Messages With Music

Conveying your promotion message, building connections of trust, and giving clarity in what you do is done best with sound and video content. Online recordings, online sounds, digital broadcasts, CDs, and DVDs are the mediums that convey your advertising messages superior to content alone. A few people like to pursue, yet everybody wants to watch and tune in, so give your advertising messages for your business in all modalities imaginable.

Yet, with regards to sound and video messages, regardless of whether it is advertising or relationship building content, the utilization of music will upgrade what is said and make an underscore to underline the word and the appreciation of the watcher is drastically improved, which means more will comprehend and react when music is appropriately utilized.

Tip 1. You should utilize music that you reserve the privileges to utilize. You can't take a CD of motion picture music or a prominent melody and use it in your advertising messages. The expense of authorizing well known and popular music isn't doable except promoters with the spending limits to manage the cost of those copyrights. There are bounty assets to acquire what is called eminence free music or purchase out music to keep it legitimate.

Tip 2. Music conveys temperaments and feelings, and most sovereignty their suppliers order free music by the emotions the music can make in individuals. So when building a message or video creation, you should guide out how you need individuals to feel while they are hearing your verbal news and seeing the visuals. Sentiments of energy, concern, parody, area, time of the season, and numerous different states of mind might be underscored by picking the correct music. So consider how you need your group of spectators to feel when they view or tune in to what you need to state.

Tip 3. Use programming that enables you to blend the volume dimensions of the music and up or down to accentuate your message when needed. The music can be felt, yet be delicate so portrayal can be heard, yet they come up more intense to change or connote and end of a critical point. PC programming enables you to review this well before you distribute, and numerous incredible projects will allow you to have full oversight of your sound blending.

National sponsors on radio, television, and web, and programming of various kinds use music because the crowds need to expect that implies proficient creation esteem generally. Individuals don't usually know why, yet they contrast your creations with the mediums what they have seen and heard on the radio, and TV for quite a long time. So when you include music and include it successfully, you raise your generation esteems nearer to levels set by those makers of radio and TV content.

The uplifting news is with the PC programming of today, stock video sites and eminence free music... superb generation esteems have never been simpler or less expensive to make. Everybody can take an interest in making convincing advertising messages for their organizations on the web and disconnected.

Web Marketing Via Royalty Free Music

Organizations around the globe are making up for lost time with the fever of Internet advertising or e-showcasing to achieve their potential clients and in this manner, increment their client base. They are embracing a few procedures of internet promoting including Search Engine Optimization (SEO), Social Media Marketing (SMM), Search Engine Marketing (SEM), Affiliate Marketing, Referral Marketing and email showcasing. Their advertising endeavors contribute significantly to their month to month costs. One additionally advertising system is demonstrating its value for various businesses both on the web and disconnected is the utilization of eminence free music in your website pages. The most significant bit of leeway of this procedure over numerous other advertising methods is that it is very reasonable as you pay for it just once and use it for a few numbers of times.

Utilizing a bit of music in your site, particularly on your landing page has turned into a pattern in the cutting edge online world. For the individuals who are curious about, everything it means is to add ambient melodies to at least one site page/s in your site. The aftereffect of doing as such is that when the client opens the website page, the music begins off. Even though this wonder has been being used for a couple of years, its fame and advantages have just been acknowledged at this point. Numerous sites have demonstrated that the utilization of eminence free music holds the watchers for more extended periods.

At whatever point you go to a café, shopping center, or travel by an extravagance train, some mood melodies continues channeling. This adds amusing to your eating, shopping, and voyaging knowledge. Thus, the motivation behind sovereignty free music installed in pages is to keep the viewers engaged and stuck to the site as far as might be feasible. In any case, clients must note a couple of significant contemplations fundamental for utilizing mood melodies in your website. A considerable number of Internet clients don't welcome the unexpected beginning of music when they open a page. A superior thought is to give them a chance to choose if they wish to hear it or not. This is conceivable by providing them an alternative to turning it on/off according to their inclination. This is particularly significant for individuals who access your site from the office or library, where they would not have any desire to make aggravation unexpectedly and welcome anger of others. Many home clients additionally don't want to hear loud music on sites.

Another worry is the motivation behind your site, the sort of data, items, and administrations you are an offer, and you're focused on spectators. If your website is about diversion and fun, at that point sovereignty free music installed on your website will make a great deal of significant worth expansion to it. Similarly vital is to pick the music cautiously, so it is in beat with your site and contributions as well. Also, the music ought to be of high caliber and energizing enough to incite the enthusiasm of guests to such an extent that they appreciate tuning in to it as opposed to hear it off. You can browse rap, piano, pop, jazz, corporate and so on.

Online Affiliate Marketing Jobs in Music Can Make Great Marketing Careers in Music

Online affiliate promoting occupations in music can make incredible advertising careers in music. To begin with, I will clarify what online branch showcasing is, and afterward, I will reveal to you how your musical foundation and gifts can make for extraordinary music related vocation in this field.

Online affiliate promoting is a generally new showcasing field yet can make extraordinary advertising employment in music. It enables the person to take an interest in online selling of items and administrations that are sold by other online organizations. There are a great many online organizations that are looking for affiliate advertisers to enable them to build their online deals. These online organizations complete billions of dollars in online sales every year. With every transaction that you take an interest in by driving clients to the dealer's site, pays you a commission, for the most part, 5% to 75% of the selling cost of the item or administration. A large number of these online organizations likewise pay you a moment level commission. That implies, every client you drive to a vendor's site based on your personal preference, you will also get commissions on every one of the special buys that client makes later on. As there are a large number of

38

online organizations, there are additionally infinite quantities of people only like you making a considerable number of dollars a month to month in this energizing field. You can be one of them by utilizing your experience in music to do something very similar in the music end of online affiliate promoting.

Presently, we should return to making promoting employment in music just as making long haul advertising careers in harmony inside the online affiliate showcasing field. There are numerous territories in this profession field that can outfit incredible promoting employment in music. You can pick one of them or the same number of as you might want. Offers of musical gear, musical instruments, music books, sheet music, CD's, musical DVDs, CD and DVD players, hardware, artistic programming, show tickets, tickets for musical plays, and so on., are for the most part zones that have music-related online vendors searching for online affiliate music advertisers. There are likewise voyage vacation bundles that have musical subjects for daily entertainment. A large portion of these voyage lines also has online affiliate showcasing programs in which you can take an interest. You may likewise take an interest in other online affiliate advertising programs in which you have learning or experience, for example, cooking, composing, carpentry, sports, outdoors, climbing or any region based on your personal preference. There are online vendors in basically all territories that would be restless for you to join with their affiliate program.

As officially expressed, the online affiliate advertising field can be begun low maintenance, full-time or even related to another music profession bearing. Numerous affiliates do undertake low maintenance and construct their organizations over the long haul. When you are as yet an understudy, this is an astounding path for you to get required as it permits you an opportunity to learn and assemble your business and afterward upon graduation you are prepared to go full-time If you so want. In any case, if you are ready to get included full-time now, you can most likely be ready for action in possibly 14 days. Regardless, you deserve to look at this energizing music advertising field.

The Top Music Related Careers and How to Obtain Them

Numerous individuals want to acquire music-related careers. With regards to having an occupation in the music business, there are a few distinct alternatives. While diverse in the music business have abilities in singing, musical instruments, or melody composing, not all jobs require or need such skills. All music entertainment careers require exertion and work to get.

One of the most astounding paying music entertainment careers is a music maker. Music makers are the leader of the music recording session. They assume responsibility with regards to music blending and altering.

Craftsman administrators likewise do well when it comes to compensation in the music business. The craftsman chief is the imagination behind the craftsman. This incorporates the exhibition and set at shows.

A sound specialist likewise conveys significant weight. The sound specialist is at live occasions to guarantee and make voice and audio effects. The specialist works previously and during the show to catch the best acoustics for the exhibition and sound of the craftsmen.

Notwithstanding these behind the scene occupations, the specialists and musicians that perform are the most well-known and wanted position by society. The craftsman supplies the musical ability as an instrument as well as voice. At times, the craftsman additionally provides the songwriting ability and thoughts for the show.

When hoping to get one of these occupations, you will probably confront the most focused field available. Regardless of whether you need to be in the spotlight or the background, there are a few hints to use to get your foot in the entryway for music-related careers.

To begin with, decide your territories of solidarity and choose where you fit in the realm of music. Do you have musical instrument ability, melody composing capacities, an incredible voice, experience blending and altering music, or innovativeness in planning sets or music names? Discover your place and work toward looking through music entertainment careers that will give you a chance to sparkle.

When you realize what region you have to move in the direction of, become more acquainted with individuals. Acquaint yourself with everyone. Get your name out in the music world. Go to whatever number of music-related capacities as could be allowed. Utilize the majority of your contacts to excel.

Settle for what you can get. Never turn down an offer of employment because of the absence of cash or acclaim. A great many people in fruitful music-related careers start little. If necessary, begin as a wedding artist, a back-up artist, music exercise instructor, or music radio representative. Consider every activity that you take as an incredible potential to being found.

Utilize all selling choices conceivably. Try not to consider a significant name record name as your individual choice. Make your very own CDs or CD fronts and sell them through online destinations, blessing stores, and some other inventive spot you can discover.

Think about a degree. While becoming wildly successful in music does not require instruction, a degree can't hurt. Pick a degree that upgrades your quality. Select a music degree, structuring degree, the board degree, or mechanical degree. Work on your instruction while you take a shot at getting your way into music-related careers.

Promoting Music Online - Getting Started With Social Media

Above all else, one of the main things you ought to do in advancing your music online is making your music available and building up an online nearness. That way, individuals will begin to realize that they exist. Regardless of whether they hear your music or not is another issue. However, as long as it's accessible, should somebody make a suggestion, they can undoubtedly discover your work. At that point, you can concentrate on advancing it.

An incredible method for doing this is by agreeing to accept a profile page on another website, for example, an internet-based life webpage, where you can include tests of your music for individuals to tune in to on the web. Indeed, even those interpersonal interaction locales that don't permit music transfers will demonstrate to be valuable.

Joining with person to person communication destinations, for example, MySpace or SoundClick is incredible for making an association with new potential fans yet enormous locales, for example, this frequently pursue patterns. They can finish up ending up so gigantic and well known with spammers who need to exploit what can be picked up from such introduction that individuals quit utilizing it and it rapidly turns into a relic of days gone by with generally spammers remaining.

Attempt to remain on the ball and sign up for records on various diverse internet-based life locales so that should the webpage go down you haven't lost the majority of your diligent work. That as well as along these lines, you can likewise observe which locales are working best for you and spotlight your time and consideration on these.

A system with, however, many related individuals as could be expected under the circumstances. By 'related' I mean individuals that are inside the equivalent or similar industry to you. Marks, A&R, musicians, bands, local devotees of that type, etc. make yourself known to the general population that issue. Don't merely include anybody as a companion. It's far-fetched they'll be of much assistance, and in case you're pushing your music to them, they in all probability won't be intrigued. Focus on the contacts and fans that have some enthusiasm for what you do as they are well on the way to really 'tune in' to your music and messages. Visually impaired showcasing won't function admirably.

So those are a portion of the essentials to advancing your music web-based utilizing online life destinations. They are essential - yet also, principal - steps that you should take if you are to begin developing your work adequately. Presently your music is online you can start chipping away at improving it in different ways and get your music heard more by the online mass of ears and battle through the online celebration of rivalry.

For what reason Is Social Media Important in Music?

We, as a whole, realize that online networking is a hugely available mode for staying in contact with devotees, yet it is significantly more than that.

These days online life stages offer free promotion, an approach to connect with new clients, networking openings, and SEO benefits.

Most importantly let's take a gander at the upsides of augmenting the advantages of internet-based life:

- Increase fans
- Get radio play
- Get some answers concerning rivalries.
- Free advancement
- Gig appointments
- Acquire profitable industry contacts

furthermore, substantially more...

We're going to make you stride by-venture through the two central locales (Facebook and Twitter), at that point include it a couple of additional ones like Digg and Reddit, that can give large lifts to a readership if you approach everything correctly.

Twitter

Twitter is an unquestionable requirement for musicians, in addition to the fact that it contains your fans, it contains record names, music celebration coordinators, scenes, radio stations - basically whoever you could envision in the business will probably have a twitter account. Presently you realize that you can utilize the accompanying approaches to benefit from it:

1 Twitterfall

Twitterfall is a site that enables you to scan for explicit terms in explicit territories. It fundamentally channels the tweets from all around the world into the precise words you're searching for.

If including a quest "with the expectation of complimentary music advancement," the tweets would sift through one by one, with the tweet and the client's profile subtleties.

Think carefully with the inquiry term; you can likewise set geolocation if you needed to scan for "bands accessible" in "London" for instance. The extraordinary thing about this is you can also spare your inquiries, include avoidances and hold returning for quite a while to new tweets from various clients.

2 Twellow

Oneself announced business index of Twitter.

You can look inside specific enterprises for individuals that identify with your industry. For our motivations, we will search inside Music and afterward the subcategory of Record Labels.

This gives a rundown of Twitter clients who are included with record marks from around the globe - you would then be able to alter this down to individuals close to your area, giving you a nice rundown of essential to pursue and maybe drop a quick message telling them about your identity and what you do.

Furthermore, also you can add yourself to the twellow registries for nothing, with the goal that when individuals search for musicians in the state the London zone there, you are!

3 Tweetdeck

Tweetdeck is a downloadable app that is overly helpful at tailing others, looking for patterns, informing individuals effortlessly and fundamentally offers a composed variant of twitter.

With the application you can redo sections to demonstrate your tweets, the tweets of others, direct messages, worldwide quests, utilize numerous records, plan your tweets and substantially more - it's mostly an online twitter form of a swiss armed force blade.

Hootsuite is a comparative gadget to Tweetdeck, and favored by a few - so make sure to look at them both.

Facebook

Each artisan and band that is around ought to have a Facebook page (And most likely as of now does).

It's taken over from MySpace as the first stop for bands on a social medium, and while MySpace still has a spot, the enormous development of locales, for example, Soundcloud and the gigantic utilization of Facebook implies that it's the first spot to keep your fans refreshed.

1 Create a fan page

Truly self-evident, yet you ought to dependably make a page for yourself or your band. In addition to the fact that it keeps it separate from your own life, it's additionally somewhat more expert and permits you to follow all sorts of things, (for example, your week by week achieve, what posts pattern well, and so forth). You can likewise make an advertisement effectively when you so want.

2 Update your photos

Since the presentation of the course of events, pictures are critical on Facebook band pages. A beautiful cover photograph is a top of the page eye getting component to a page.

3 Add Apps

FBML is an extraordinary application which enables you to include HTML code (or some of it) to an area of your Facebook page. You can either approach this in one of two different ways - from an SEO viewpoint by adding connects to various pieces of your site (including more backlinks from a decent source), or add links to music, pictures and make a quite looking segment to your page.

There are bunches of different applications out there to add to your page; these are continually evolving. For instance, BandPage is one to take a gander at to include a BandPage... however, due to applications continuously transforming, you may need to Google for the best ones out there.

4 Integrate with Spotify

Spotify has moved toward becoming number one approach to tuning in to music lawfully. It is an incredible administration and has helped overcome any issues between illegal downloading and gushing to legitimate web use.

Coordinate your Facebook page with your Spotify represent the full advantages of Spotify!

Keep Your Readers Entertained

Presently you realize approaches to improve the online networking background you have to offer them something! Currently, while this isn't an exact science and indeed includes a touch of experimentation, there are some incredible models out there of how to keep your fans engaged and returning for additional:

Post Pictures

Posting pictures will give yourselves a distinct edge over the challenge. We're not merely discussing gigs; we're talking about you strolling hound, or going bungee bouncing, a sort of off-camera take a gander at the life of your band.

Offer a free download of a melody for a retweet.

Bands have begun doing this with great achievement. If you have a tune you're willing to offer for nothing; you can contact a broad group of spectators. Retweet link is a case of how to approach this.

Give a lot of shoutouts.

Connect with supporters however much as could reasonably be expected, utilize the stunning @ key to yell out to individuals and make them talk.

Additional Social Mediums

Reddit and Digg are among my preferred destinations for music advancement and can help increase vast quantities of guests - to an intriguing source.

Individuals regularly approach Reddit and Digg in the incorrect manner, attempting to propel themselves in to an open online chasm, though it should be considered more to be a discourse gathering where if something is precious, unusual and intriguing it will get a lot of perspectives, be shared and add a ton of capacity to your webpage from an SEO viewpoint.

To summarise make sure to refresh your social pages, utilize the stunning applications out there to pick up fans, contact individuals in the business, and quest for valuable data. At that point share photographs, fascinating web journals and stories to your fans and mingle these on destinations, for example, Digg and Reddit for an additional reaction.

It requires investment, yet the advantages of doing as such causes you acquire fans, yet also, assemble yourself/your band as a brand, which is critical in the advanced age.

PR For Musicians

Maybe the most challenging inquiry that a musician needs to answer with regards to public relations or to showcase is - why? Isn't having made the craftsmanship enough? The short response to that is no and especially not presently. If you need to achieve your public and get your craft presentation, you have to assume responsibility for your promoting and your profession. This is especially valid in the music world. The business has been flipped around. The times of name propelled vocations are everything except a memory. In truth, musicians ought to have dependably been engaged with their showcasing and advancement, however at this point, with the seismic movements occurring, it has turned into a need

The terrible news is that when you need to dispatch a fruitful vocation, you have to figure out how to advertise yourself. Fortunately, this is an entirely different world and one wherein you can have more control of your showcasing, your picture, and your specialty than any time in recent memory.

There are a heap approaches to advance yourself, from such old benchmarks as flyers and postcards, to promotions, public relations, online showcasing and web-based social networking. For structure a picture and an individual brand, PR remains the best and approving type of advancement. Through public relations, you become the news. It's the primary type of promoting that can achieve your objective market and offer believability and approval. Consider it, if you somehow managed to peruse a promotion for a musician in a newspaper, or read an article profiling that musician in a similar paper, which would catch your eye? One is a paid advertisement; the other is a news story. Which would you be bound to accept?

With the intensity of online promoting and web-based life, PR campaigns could easily compare to ever. Joined with an online networking campaign, public relations takes on an entirely different look. The vast majority consider PR to be online life as an "either/or" decision, where it should be an "and" choice.

Even though YouTube, Twitter, FaceBook, MySpace were enormous Internet stories, they wound up worldwide powerhouses as a result of conventional media inclusion in such outlets as CNN, the Today Show, the New York Times, Time magazine and the Wall Street Journal. The legend is that everything happens online, where really, it's the following procedure. These accounts begin online. They develop and frequently develop in a significant manner. However, the tales genuinely detonate after the predominant press covers them. The media inclusion drives the online title wave.

Others at that point attempt to repeat the marvels on the Internet, not understanding that they forget the most significant component - PR, directed media inclusion on a standard TV and in real newspapers and magazines. Since online promoting and internet-based life are still generally new and convincing, most miss the PR part of the showcasing condition.

However, before you can bounce to showcasing yourself, you need to deal with the essentials and gain proficiency with the craft of PR. Recall that, you will prevail by figuring out how the media thinks, not by accepting you realize what they need. Coming up next are a few hints that can ideally build your P.R.

Characterize your story and your vocation way. You can't inform others regarding what you do until you completely comprehend it yourself. Compose a short and the small section that characterizes what you do. Compose it with the goal that an eighth grader could get it. You might be astonished.

Characterize your objective market.

Think as far as stories. Individuals comprehend ideas best when recounted regarding narrative stories.

Compose a reasonable, brief one-page press discharge.

Concentrate the different media outlets. Tailor your discharges and your pitches to every particular media outlet.

Toning it down would be ideal. In case you're considering conveying a gigantic press unit loaded up with reams of paper, photographs, and leaflets, reconsider.

Inspect the majority of the accessible edges. Your first pitch may not work. Be inventive.

Learn tolerance, be persevering, and get ready for progress. This is the hardest idea to ace. We've had campaigns that have hit a grand slam in the first week. However, most require some serious energy and constancy.

Public relations is a moderate structure, on-going, total procedure. When you are going to execute a P.R. campaign, pledge to remain with it for at least a half year. It will be justified, despite all the trouble. Your vocation will be happy you did.

The Function Musician - Online Promotion and Marketing for Musicians

As a guitarist for the contract at weddings and occasions, I might want to share my experience of the showcasing side of things with regards to being an independent musician. There are numerous approaches to advance yourself in this genuinely jam-packed market, and beneath is a rundown of the more powerful courses...

1. Fabricate A Website

The conspicuous central center for your online advancement. There are two perspectives to making a reliable website:

Content.

The content should enamor and preservationist, as it were very elegantly composed, no outcry marks, swear words, etc. Your sound/video demos should be available from the landing page, and ideally, start-up consequently on passage to the site. Past customer tributes are an absolute necessity. Set records ought to be masterminded by type, and as tremendous as could be allowed.

It is conceivable to make a website yourself through a website layout administration, or you can utilize a website specialist.

Website improvement (SEO).

This is how your website positions in the web indexes and numerous variables are deciding the result. One factor is content - a straightforward guide is self-evident; if a potential customer types a pursuit inquiry into Google and so forth, how pertinent would the content on your website be? It is critical to recognize significant catchphrases and expressions and spot them deliberately in different pieces of your website, the original content as well as in page titles, picture subtitles, etc. The other primary consideration in quality SEO is your webpage's backlinks - the number of connections on other essential and quality websites indicating your website. Subsequently, a noteworthy continuous undertaking is third-party referencing, by enlisting your link on different websites. There are various great sources to start, for example, neighborhood/musician registries.

There are numerous great instructional exercises on SEO for novices found through the web indexes. Go for the top positioning ones, and they comprehend what they're doing.

2. Register With Musician Agencies

Numerous quality music offices in the UK acknowledge craftsman applications. Whenever, the office will request music/video, photographs, and a short history together with customer tributes.

Most offices are allowed to join and take a rate commission charge for each gig they book for you.

3. Web-based life

It is essential nowadays to set up and keep up internet-based life pages, just because of how individuals go about as 'buyers' has changed; individuals request association and consideration before resolving to buys. Facebook, Twitter, YouTube, and different destinations should have your subtleties, and each page should point to your first website. For instance, I utilize my Facebook page to gather other Facebook customer tributes, and these fill in as a certifiable wellspring of positive remarks on my exhibitions. Each time I connect with a Facebook 'fan' I contact the companions of the fan, expanding introduction in a characteristic without cost way.

4. Promoting

To truly move over the challenge here and there a little speculation is required. There are a couple of alternatives for the capacity musician to investigate...

Google AdWords - pay per snap promoting from list items.

Facebook Advertising - pay per click/1000 impressions focusing on various socioeconomics.

Authority indexes/magazines - e.g., wedding registries.

Selling Music: How Musicians Can Make Money Online

The notoriety of the Internet has offered to ascend to a new age of autonomous experts profiting online, and musicians aren't an exemption. If you are taking a gander at selling music, this article clarifies three of the numerous ways musicians can profit online.

Make tracks sell for sovereignties.

The first and most clear method for profiting online with music is by making tracks that can later be sold. The Internet makes it simple to independently publish and build a following without the support of a music mark. When you need to go this course pursue on the strides of online music, big names and distribute your video on YouTube, make a

Facebook page, and grasp internet-based life advancement to get fans through viral promoting. Administrations, for example, Spotify or iTunes enable autonomous artisans to sell their music and can be an extraordinary wellspring of presentation, however, as a matter of fact, the eminences won't approach those appreciated by prominent specialists, and you may need to pay around $10 forthright to get your tracks online.

Give music administrations, for example, the soundtrack for promotion

An ever-increasing number of individuals need specially designed music tracks as a foundation for online video advertisements, organization introductions or even things, for example, wedding photography. It merits investigating entering associations with media or publicizing offices or other autonomous experts, for example, picture takers or producers. Another zone to investigate is soundtracks for free short movies: While the cash may not be incredible, the introduction can be shockingly high, and it's the sort of imaginative undertaking numerous musicians love.

YouTube recordings and promotion or memberships

Another method for profiting online with your music is by adapting your music recordings, on stage, for example, YouTube. A few fronts of famous tunes played with remarkable expertise or in a specific particular manner have a large number of online visits and can be adapted at the snap of a catch. Another route for musicians to profit online is by making educative recordings and either changing them through publicizing or by selling a membership. An ever-increasing number of individuals are going to the Internet to figure out how to get things done, and quality educational material can be an incredible wellspring of customary pay.

The Internet isn't useful for selling your music, yet it is additionally an excellent spot to share or purchase beats to make your perfect melodic work of art. Musicians who go online will locate that getting comfortable with online music dissemination apparatuses it's commendable speculation of their time and can turn out to be entirely beneficial.

CHAPTER THREE

Online Branding for Musicians How to - Why Branding Your Band Is Essential

YOUR LOGO:

This is most likely the least complicated type of image. Each demonstration ought to have a logo that somehow or another or another speaks to your identity. It ought to be straightforward and straightforward. In any case, you should have one. Try not to surge it - do a wide range of thoughts and tests until you pick the last form. Work together with band-individuals, fans, and companions for various ideas. Six heads are superior to one.

YOUR STORY:

Keep in mind; you need your digital image to recount to the narrative of your identity. Concentrate on subtleties that depict your picture and resemblance, your dramatic reliable look, and a predictable look and feel for your sites and online networking. When you devise your marked map, misuse it all over the place. At the point when fans move from site to site or see you play out, your image must be steady.

Wherever individuals search for you, they should most likely know it's you - mostly by observing your reliable logo, brand, and picture. It must be essential!!

Build A COMMUNITY OF FOLLOWERS:

Customize your fan commitment encounters. Construct trust and friendship in your nearby close to a home network. Connect as regularly as could be allowed. Perhaps use brand-infused giveaways as an approach to expand your supporter's cooperation.

Use Instagram, Twitter, and Facebook to spread your image and open it too continually; however, many devotees as could be expected under the circumstances. Shoot proficient recordings. The video will improve your vision and give your fans a more intensive see what you're about and turned out to be nearer to you.

Eclipse YOUR COMPETITION:

Rule your specific music advertise by being particular in each part of your digital and conventional promoting endeavors. A few models are your official site, your web-based life destinations and posts, new CD discharges, and particularly in your merchandise. Your merch must be particular and express your picture and brand in its designs. Alongside your logo, merch designs ought to likewise mirror your band's character and its general story. The plans ought to be unique and stylish. When they're cool designs, individuals will get them regardless of whether it had nothing to do with your band; henceforth, progressively insurance presentation for your image.

Attention and MUSIC MEDIA RELATIONS:

Adventure your image in the news media, meetings, radio, and in music audit websites. Getting inclusion in any of the media outlets will make genuine consideration and mindfulness for your image, and further upgrade it. This kind of effort is better-taken care of by a prepared music marketing expert. It requires a lot of investment, ability, and a gathering of prominent media contacts. It's amazingly hard for the usual craftsman to be paid attention to by media outlets. An expert music marketing specialist, who is trusted by the media, may cost you a couple of bucks, yet it merits each penny.

Along these lines, IN SUMMARY:

Keep in mind, don't get excessively exceptional or confounded. What's more, above all, don't get disappointed. Take as much time as necessary - do it right and keep it basic. Remember to work with the majority of your band-individuals, fans, companions, and supporters with regards to building up your logo, story, picture, and designs. Six heads are superior to one. Investigate the very prevalent acts that you appreciate - perceive how they approach marking. You might need to consider copying a portion of their thoughts.

Marking is not kidding business. It's not something to be overlooked. It's the visual portrayal of you as a craftsman. Have a fabulous time, and do it!

RSS, A Good Alternative for Musicians

If you are an individual from a band, a performance craftsman, maker or an individual associated with the music world somehow, you know that individuals need to think about the work you are doing before getting to be fans. For musicians, the music itself is the intention to spread their work and feeling. However, they likewise need to be composed to contact the potential group of spectators they need.

For musicians, RSS is a superb option because it tends to be used in two unique ways; update planned fans about the present and forthcoming exercises, and communicate news for recently discharged sound or video material. In this way, setting up an official page is the initial step to being making the stage you have to succeed, trailed by setting up a blog and web recording bolsters.

Blog feeds are created consequently every time you, or a staff part, post an update about musical exercises or those tasks that you have as a top priority. Digital recording encourages, then again, help you to convey non-standard music, syndicated programs, or records that generally may not achieve your blog group of spectators or the average user surfing the web for music refreshes.

Like some other type of syndication, RSS channels for music substance can be likewise shared and conveyed among different musicians, makers, or sites dedicated to communicating news on the music and media outlet. RSS is additionally a savvy instrument for mass appropriation with regards to promoting efforts.

Online music has made conceivable far-reaching enthusiasm for musical updates, so whether you are beginning your music vocation or a long stroll behind you, RSS will add to start assembling you're a fan.

Podcasting comprises disseminating digital multimedia files on the Internet for downloading, so you can draw in incalculable audience members with the guide of RSS.

Also, web recordings make conceivable sell segments of your musical work, and furthermore may fill in as demos for makers looking for new ability yet how might you contact them? Unmistakably the best approach is Simple Syndication (RSS.)

All things considered, in the event that you spend at some point completing a little research, you will discover numerous examples of overcoming adversity depicting musicians who broke into the standard in the wake of discharging a solitary by means of digital broadcast, or got a chronicle contract after a music industry master bought in to a band's RSS refreshes.

How To Gain Music Fans And Build Promoting Skills

Okay, prefer to realize how to acquire music fans? Do you wish you knew the key to building a tremendous after? OK, prefer to achieve the ideal approach to advance yourself as a musician? When you need to make enduring progress in the music business, it is significant that you have a lot of devoted fans who are keen on what you do as a musician. To do this, you should gain proficiency with the best techniques for advancing both yourself and your music.

In any case, the response to "How would I get more fans and advance my music vocation?" isn't effectively found by adopting an exceedingly summed up strategy that 'appears' to work for different musicians. At some random minute, you (or the band you play in) might battle with various extraordinary difficulties that would necessitate that you take specific activities to get more fans or reinforce your limited time endeavors. Regardless of where you are in your music profession and what difficulties you face, you have three objectives to accomplish when you need to both increase more music fans and advance your music:

You need to get more individuals to look at your music.

When somebody tunes in to your music, you need them to help bolster you in some way (purchasing your collections, watching you live, buying any product, and so on.)

You have to change your fans into absolute aficionados who will utilize the informal exchange to enlighten every one of their companions concerning you and your music.

Regardless of what it is that you are attempting to accomplish in the music business, the three objectives referenced above will apply to anything you do as long as you are trying to build up a stable association with your fans.

These objectives may all appear to be isolated from each other; they are in actuality all associated. When you can make progress with any single one of them, you will significantly improve your odds for development with any of the others. When you really 'get' this fundamental truth, you will think that it's a lot simpler to be beneficial in your endeavors.

To make extraordinary progress as you elevate your music to your fans, you should figure out how to think in a critical way instead of merely taking conflicting and segregated activities (a slip-up that most musicians and groups make). Rather than attempting to locate a general equation that you can apply to enable you to get more fans for your music, you have to start thinking similarly as most expert musicians. While preparing different musicians to prevail in their music vocations, I help them see how to discover imaginative thoughts that they can apply in their very own music profession to rapidly acquire music fans. When you gain the capacity to think like this in your very own music vocation, it will turn out to be a lot simpler for you to beat any hindrances that hinder your limited time endeavors.

To show what I mean and give you different advances (that you can take right currently to get more music fans), here are some fast and simple things you can do to achieve each of the three of the music advancement objectives referenced previously.

To get you on the way to increasing more music fans and developing your present music advancement endeavors, I will currently indicate you different things that you can do yourself to achieve the three objectives referenced previously.

Alright, since you have completed the appraisal above, keep perusing to locate a few noteworthy strides beneath that you can use to advance your music. While you are reading them, don't concentrate as much on the activities themselves; instead, think inventively to see the thoughts and thinking 'behind' the actions to comprehend why they are so powerful. This will keep you from essentially 'replicating' them and will lead you to believe of thoughts that you can profit by in your particular music vocation circumstance.

Music Promotion Action Step: Get more individuals to tune in to your music.

Arrangement #1: Join different musicians in taking an interest in a gathering CD. After you have discharged an aggregation collection, you have accomplished two or three essential things. In the first place, you have successfully created a record that contains your very own music. Second, not just have you picked up an apparatus to elevate yourself to your fans, yet you have picked up an instrument that possibly raises you to each other musician's supporters on the collection (with no extra exertion on your part). Keep in mind, the objective of this isn't to profit straightforwardly, but instead to utilize the collection as a cheap device to advance your music (and the music of different musicians) to more individuals on a bigger scale. You can likewise apply this thought as an approach to use your very own collection discharges and items to an enormous rundown of fans. "Leverage" (utilizing one activity to increase multiple advantages) is fundamental if you need to accomplish an abnormal state of achievement in your music profession. This is something I help individuals in my Music Careers Mentoring Program create and refine.

Arrangement #2: Work together with different musicians locally. Rather than believing other nearby musicians to be your opposition (for increasing more fans), cooperate with neighborhood musical specialists of a similar type to enable you to access more significant measure of fans who are keen on hearing and seeing you play music. One technique for accomplishing this is to work with another band to perform at a similar setting with an end goal to unite the fan base of the two groups. By doing this, you won't just improve your association with the proprietor of the scene (since you are getting more individuals). However, you will have the chance to publicize your music to the next band's fan base (and them to yours). This thought is exceptionally principal; however, as a general rule, relatively few groups step up and go out and do it. Also, numerous groups tragically share the scene with different groups who are not in their objective market, or with groups who don't try to pull in their fans to the setting (in this manner removing the apparent advantage). One case of pulling this thought off (which is genuinely necessary for the music business) is the point at which a band with a little after moves toward becoming an opening represent a lot bigger band. Nonetheless, if you can't discover a very successful group to open for you can, in any case, accomplish this; you should create a band that contains musicians who have enough aspiration to make a move and actualize this technique.

Music Promotion Action Step: Get your fans to take specific activities.

Arrangement #1: Make beyond any doubt that individuals have a motivating force to both be an aficionado of your music AND buy your music. The individuals who have aced the capacity to successfully elevate music discover approaches to get their fan base to purchase their music instead of downloading it online for nothing. Also, they can take a regular audience and turn him/her into an unwavering fan. An incredible method to do this is to offer something exceptional to individuals who BUY your music (that can't be gotten by just downloading it for nothing). To viably do this, it is significant that whatever you are putting forth can't be adequately replicated through advanced media. This could incorporate things, for example, VIP goes to your shows, stock, or other innovative and exciting things. The primary concern to get out this thought is that you can execute a solitary procedure to accomplish significant music advancement while additionally building up a more grounded connection among you and your fans.

Arrangement #2: Become acquainted with your existing fan base. It is anything but difficult to successfully advance yourself as a musician when you can put yourself out there to the individuals who as of now give you their help at whatever point you seek after new tasks in your musical vocation. Most musicians imagine that their most concerning issue is an absence of music fans when truth be told, they don't have a clue who their genuine fans are and how to connect with them. Rather than reaching these particular fans, a ton of musicians centers their endeavors around the overall population. Indeed, this methodology can work; nonetheless, advancing your music as such will cost a lot of cash and time. To significantly eliminate your expenses concerning money, vitality, and time; make your musical advancement increasingly successful by finding a simple method to keep in contact with your fan base consistently.

Music Promotion Action Step: Transform your present fans into FANATICS.

Arrangement #1: Put together extraordinary social occasions or occasions that drench your fans in your music and draw in them on an unheard of level (rather than simply tuning in to your music or watching you live). There an almost unlimited way for you to do this - restricted uniquely by your eagerness to be inventive. Recollect the key is to build up your association with your music fans.

Arrangement #2: Focus on rewarding your most faithful fans with one of a kind endowments that easygoing audience members don't approach. This idea can be utilized together with the principal point depicted above or as a thought independent from anyone else. If you'd like for your music fans to make a specific move (for instance carrying more individuals to your exhibitions or to buy your collections), center around discovering something of high worth that you can offer them that goes past the extent of music. (Keep in mind: Your music fans don't need free cash or shirts... consider something explicit to offer them)

As you have perused, when you adopt an increasing point by point strategy to seeing explicitly what it is that you need to do with regards to "increasing more music fans," it's much more apparent explicitly which activity steps you should perform to get this going. Most musicians consider improving their music while attempting to engage the overall population, however doing this is only a single part of musical advancement. Your music is significant; anyway, there are parts of your music vocation that you should take a shot at to get more fans for your music viable. When you start concentrating on these viewpoints, you will begin to increase a lot more prominent outcomes in your music advancement endeavors.

Independent Online Music Promotion - 6 Free Ways to Get Your Music Heard!

1. Transfer Your Music - Sounds simple enough, yet it's still a generally disregarded and ignored thought by individual musicians if you aren't transferring your music since you don't have the foggiest idea how at that point discover someone who does. It's not hard, and it's not costly. There are numerous destinations where you can do this for nothing and utilize their apparatuses. When you can use a PC, you can transfer your music. Jump on it!

2. Assemble a site or blog with pictures, music, gigs, profiles, and so forth - Again, this doesn't need to be troublesome, and you most likely know someone who can fabricate a site. It doesn't need to be extravagant, get your essence on the web. Look at your preferred musician's sites for thoughts. Fill it with your photos and give some data on you and your band. Tell individuals your identity and rundown every one of the gigs you've played and UPCOMING shows! Make a blog with the expectation of complimentary that you can refresh day by day and keep individuals educated. You can likewise begin an email mailing rundown of fans so you can tell them of gigs, discharges or anything new...instantly!

3. Jump on discussions, online journals, and different sites and spread the news about you and your band! - Visit considerations identified with your kind of music and begin getting included. Make remarks on these discussions and websites that let individuals know your identity. Make sure to make remarks that add to the debate and not merely to publicize yourself, or you might be commenced. Solicit some from your fans, loved ones to do likewise. The more individuals out there discussing you, the better.

4. Record and discharge your best songs online! - Another simple thought, however now and again you see musicians and need to think about how well they thoroughly considered this. If you will transfer your music to a social systems administration site, or your website...or both, ensure it's your best stuff. I don't think I need to go over how significant initial introductions are isn't that right?

5. Make a music video! It doesn't make a difference how modest. - Be imaginative with this one when you don't officially claim a camcorder, at that point, attempt to obtain one. This doesn't need to be a multi-million dollar video, only something to show individuals the character behind the music. It tends to be shot, altered, and transferred for no expense by any means. Get a companion to assist with the camera while you do your thing! Probably the best recordings out there have been shot by handheld cameras with no financial limit.

It descends to your enthusiasm and imagination, and once you have a video, get it transferred when you can.

6. Connection your online profiles destinations and downloads back to your locales and comparative musicians. - As we expressed in #3, you have to begin getting the message out about your music by visiting different sites and sites and making remarks. Continuously ensure that when you compose a comment on a blog or website, that you put a connection at the base of your post back to your site, video and so on.

Give individuals a chance to see that you have a nearness on the web, and they will click your connections and look at you. You can likewise exchange joins with comparable musicians to yourself. You can twofold the size of your fan base by essentially making game plans with different musicians to put interfaces on every others destination that connection back to your locales.

This is an incredible method to have your music begin appearing all once again the spot and get new fans that might not have generally known about you. It's additionally an incredible method to make companions with different musicians that can enable you to transform your music into the following substantial online hit!

There are such huge numbers of approaches to advance music online; it will make your head turn.

Step by step instructions to Promote Your Music: Building a Fanbase

For any individual getting to be engaged with the music business, it is critical that he/she set up a robust system of fans and grow profound associations with them to guarantee enduring accomplishment as a musician.

In many cases, when hopeful specialists request counsel on advancing their music, they get general directions on the best way to pick up an introduction in the music business. The accompanying will look to give you the inverse. Here are some immediate, working, and compelling techniques to advance your music.

1. Begin Performing Shows

Expecting that your music quality is as of now up to industry standard, the initial step an artisan should take to start picking up a following is performing appears. When you don't have a lot of assets, begin by performing at little settings in your neighborhood. Bit by bit construct your fanbase. You may need to play out various shows at a similar scene to start building profound associations with the "regulars" at the settings, yet it will certainly be justified regardless of your time. Informal promoting is the best type of showcasing.

As you keep on structure your neighborhood following, branch out to surrounding urban areas and perform at their scenes. Work on structure your name and brand inside your city, locale, and afterward broadly.

2. Give Out Free Samples

Giving out free downloads or free sampler CDs of your music is an incredible route for fans to get acquainted with your work. When you give out an example of your work, DO NOT JUST GIVE IT TO PEOPLE AND LEAVE. Regardless of whether you're giving your music out online or disconnected, you need to attempt to set up a type of association with your fans. Fans need to feel like they can identify with you.

3. Make A Blog Or Website

Making a blog or site around your music is an excellent method to assemble your image and fanbase online. Make sure to post a life story, discography (if accessible), connections to your music and social networks, applicable recordings, and approaches to get in touch with you. If you can expound on music related articles, surveys, or your suppositions, that will likewise be useful to you.

4. Get Social On Social Networks

Regardless of whether you are using social bookmarking sites, or have a simple Facebook profile, get effectively engaged with your social networks. When you are performing at a show, make sure to advise your group of spectators to add you to their social networks. Be available to the discussion. Attempt to fabricate stable connections online. When you add companions to your system, make sure to target individuals who may check out you and your music. Likewise, search for experts inside your class of music to check whether you can get guidance or system with them.

5. Contract A Publicist

When the assets are accessible to you, procuring a marketing expert is an extraordinary path for your addition further introduction for yourself and music. A marketing specialist can help create press inclusion for your sake just as fill in as a liaison among you and the media/open.

6. Begin An E-mailing List

Having a messaging rundown to refresh fans and supporters about your music is an extremely incredible asset! Make sure to build up one to keep your fans educated about up and coming shows, new collection discharges, media attention, and then some. Try not to Spam!

7. Overview The Public

This could be known as a musician's "distinct advantage." Input is a frequently ignored part of music advancement. Use overviews and surveys to get a thought of how the open like your music and whether your present advancement techniques are viable. Perform studies and surveys disconnected and online — additionally, attempt reviews in zones where you've performed away.

How to Promote Your Music

The most effective method to PROMOTE YOUR MUSIC WITHOUT THE INTERNET

A PLAN FOR MUSIC PROMOTION

Ordinarily, a smart thought to advance music comes in the head at the most troublesome occasions, for example, when perusing or in some fascinating spots.

The best suggestion is to purchase a scratch pad and record the ridiculously. Try not to depend on your memory. Usually, sooner or later, you overlook these considerations.

Numerous thoughts, too brief period

When you have aggregated a rundown of great, fascinating thoughts for the improvement of your vocation, think about every single imaginable approach to utilize them by and by. Most artists are lost now, not realizing where to begin, and don't do anything. Or on the other hand do, yet practically nothing, conveying just a little piece of what has been instituted. Try not to overburden yourself; attempt to be reliable. Before you start to take part in enormous scale advancement, recollect two fundamental things that should be played out each day.

1) Write, record, and make great music. It is an indisputable fact - the most splendid and innovative particular thoughts and innovation progression can't power individuals to tune in to and purchase average music. Along these lines always sharpen your compositional and idyllic ability. Make at any rate one extremely incredible tune which will as of now be sufficient to light the flame of your notoriety.

2) The second thing you have to do each day - is to make strides towards finding new audience members and increase their consideration and compassion. Attempt to improve technical abilities and discover companions in the music business, don't be occupied from the primary concern, which is to create new crowds and speak with old aficionados of your music. The importance of your work is in your audience members. The quickest method to spread your music is by listening in on others' conversations, so remember to keep a decent association with your fan base.

So detail an arrangement... an ideal arrangement... what's more, Get out and advance yourself!

HOW AND WHERE TO PROMOTE MUSIC

Give me a chance to ask you for an inquiry... What ought to befall a man, that he turns into an enthusiast of your music? This inquiry has many answers, yet most importantly - this individual ought to tune in to your music. That is the place individuals can hear your music: on the radio or TV, the Internet, in the club, a disco, a shop, a companion at home or in the vehicle or... at your concert. Focusing on the last mentioned, because, in spite of all the mechanical advances, live melodic execution - still a standout amongst the best approaches to discover the group of spectators, to sell the CD, and at last, convey what needs to be as an artist. I would trust that in your limited time showcasing plan keep a ton of live shows and perform them with certainty...

How and what shows would you say you are arranging?

The issue is that numerous artists are trapped in an endless cycle and nobody can see different conceivable outcomes for their exhibitions, except those that as of now exist. For instance, most musical gangs run like lemmings in cafés and nightclubs. Most performers playing acoustic instruments are amassed in the restaurants and swarmed places. This is fine. However, that is the place the inventiveness closes. And after that, every one of these artists has grasped that they have a couple of choices, and they state that they have no place to play. Rethink your needs about performing.

Furthermore, ask yourself the correct inquiries. If you are asking yourself, "How would I arrange more shows in clubs," at that point you are probably not going to perceive any new chances. Put it another way, for instance, "How would I carry my music to the most extreme number of perfect fans through live exhibitions?" Keep a rundown of your thoughts regarding discovering new fans and uncovering your music.

Where would you be able to play out your music before progressively potential fans? If the "dance club" is your lone answer, think further. What about open festivals, shows for inhabitants of specific territories of your city, during incredible discoveries, meetings, vehicle appears, create fairs, open shorelines on happy days... Keep your music business cards and flyers within reach. No one can tell when you will meet somebody who is intrigued by your music... or on the other hand notice board on which you can stick a pamphlet. The business card enables the other party to recall about you sooner or later after the discussion, that you should take a gander at your page, or visit the show.

Few out of every odd choice is directly for you, because of your music, and chances to sort out the critical sound, arrange sets, etc. However, anything whatever strikes a chord on where to give a show, you ought to consider cautiously - the perfect highlights may not be apparent at first look. It is helpful to pursue this appeal since a couple of artists in such abnormal spots. So you will have next to no challenge as far as exhibitions, contrasted with similar clubs that have numerous artists arranging at their doorstep for an opportunity to perform. Dependably make sure to play at each chance you get. This is the most straightforward approach to get your music uncovered. Who knows? Perhaps a delegate of a record mark will hear your music at the most surprising time.

So... grow the capacities of your live exhibitions, ask yourself inquiries and you will see numerous better approaches to discover a considerable number of fans through shows.

CONCLUSION

If you need to realize how to advance your music and get music contracts, you may feel like you've hit an impasse. Possibly you've been playing with your band for a spell. Perhaps you even have a nearby after and everybody appears to adore your music and has a decent time at your shows. In any case, if you need to become wildly successful in the music business, it can feel like a wet dream. You need it to occur, and you want to make music your full-time enthusiasm... how would you arrive?

The music business appears as though it's loaded with mysteries and insiders, and nobody needs to give newcomer access. Of course, you hear tales about groups or performers who are found on YouTube and marked to million dollar music contracts. You can even catch wind of a neighborhood band who plays the correct gig and out of the blue is offered a record bargain. If you've been attempting to get your brand out there and trying to advance your music, when is that going to transpire? Do you genuinely require a "major break" to make it in the music business and score music contracts?

When it appears as though you need nothing but karma to get marked to a record name, it can feel defeating. To what extent can you indeed continue doing likewise again and again and still want to do it? Regardless of whether music is your life and you would prefer not to do whatever else, it can get old playing similar settings end of the week after the conclusion of the week. So what would it be advisable for you to do?

You certainly need an arrangement. What's more, it begins with treating your music, and how to advance your music and band, as a business. Indeed, music can be fun, yet if you need to get marked and you are worn out on looking out for lightning to strike, it's an excellent opportunity to quit fooling around.

www.ingramcontent.com/pod-product-compliance
Lightning Source LLC
Chambersburg PA
CBHW072200170526
45158CB00004BB/1717